Show Tunes
Accordion Songbook

Contents

Another Suitcase In Another Hall *Evita* **4**
Anthem *Chess* **7**
Cabaret *Cabaret* **10**
Can't Help Lovin' Dat Man *Showboat* **15**
Consider Yourself *Oliver!* **18**
Climb Ev'ry Mountain *The Sound Of Music* **21**
Hello, Young Lovers *The King And I* **36**
Ol' Man River *Showboat* **24**
Seventy Six Trombones *The Music Man* **28**
Till There Was You *The Music Man* **41**
What I Did For Love *A Chorus Line* **46**

Wise Publications
London/New York/Paris/Sydney/Copenhagen/Berlin/Madrid/Hong Kong/Tokyo

Exclusive Distributors:

Music Sales Limited
14-15 Berners Street,
London W1T 3LJ, UK.

Music Sales Pty Limited
20 Resolution Drive,
Caringbah, NSW 2229,
Australia.

Order No. AM951093
ISBN 978-0-7119-7093-9
This book © Copyright 1998 by Wise Publications

Unauthorised reproduction of any part of this publication by any means including
photocopying is an infringement of copyright.

Book design by Chloë Alexander
Compiled by Peter Evans
Music arranged by Pete Lee
Music processed by Enigma Music Production Services

Printed in the EU.

Cover photography by George Taylor
Instrument featured: Trevani Francesco, made in Castelfidardo, Italy
by Guerrini & Figli. Kindly loaned by Trevani, 14 Mapledale Avenue,
Croydon CR0 5TB, UK.
Cover photograph of *The King & I* courtesy of Performing Arts Library

Your Guarantee of Quality
As publishers, we strive to produce every book to the highest commercial standards.
The music has been freshly engraved and the book has been carefully designed to minimise
awkward page turns and to make playing from it a real pleasure.
Particular care has been given to specifying acid-free, neutral-sized paper made from pulps
which have not been elemental chlorine bleached. This pulp is from farmed sustainable
forests and was produced with special regard for the environment.
Throughout, the printing and binding have been planned to ensure a sturdy, attractive
publication which should give years of enjoyment.
If your copy fails to meet our high standards, please inform us and we will gladly replace it.

www.musicsales.com

Another Suitcase In Another Hall
Music by Andrew Lloyd Webber ◆ Lyrics by Tim Rice

Slowly ♩ = 90

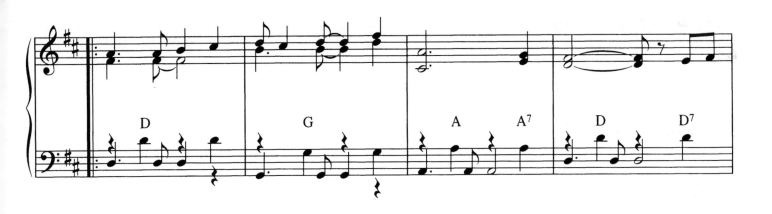

© Copyright 1976 & 1977 Evita Music Limited.
This Arrangement © Copyright 1998 Evita Music Limited.
All Rights Reserved. International Copyright Secured.

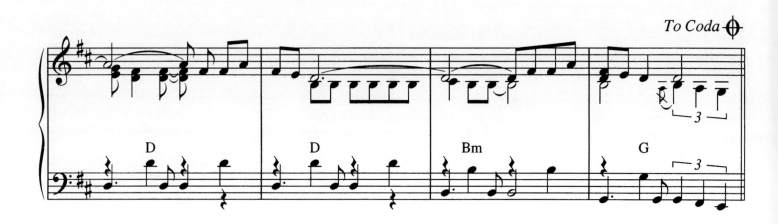

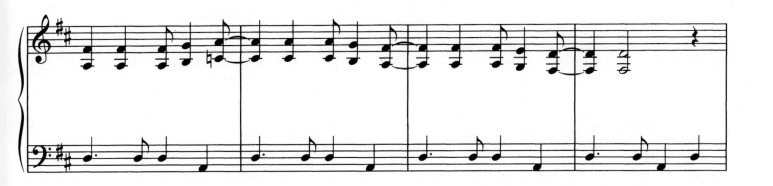

Anthem
Words & Music by Benny Andersson, Tim Rice & Bjorn Ulvaeus

© Copyright 1984 3 Knights Limited. Copyright administered for the world by Union Songs AB, Stockholm, Sweden.
PolyGram International Music Publishing Limited, 8 St. James Square, London W1.
All Rights Reserved. International Copyright Secured.

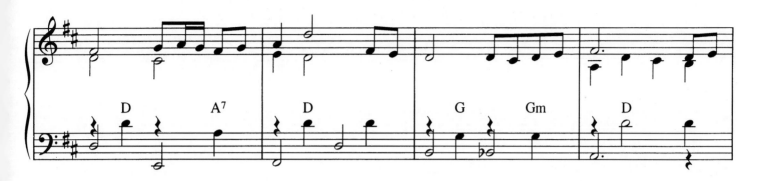

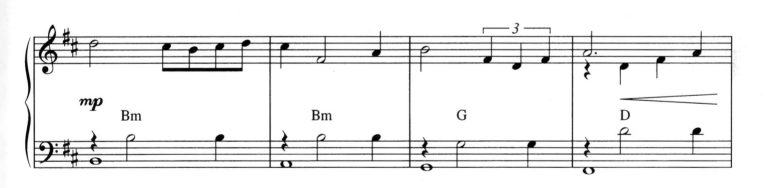
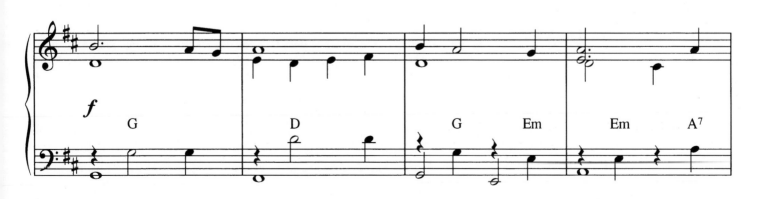

7

Cabaret
Music by John Kander ◆ Lyrics by Fred Ebb

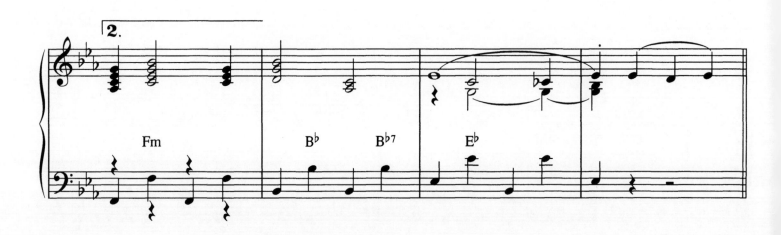
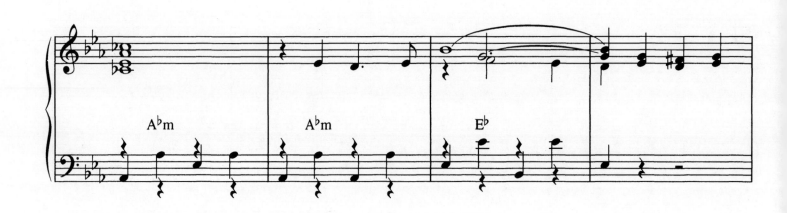

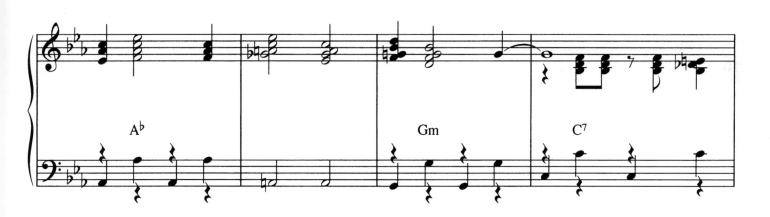
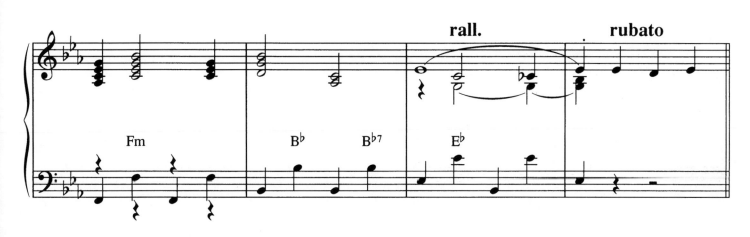

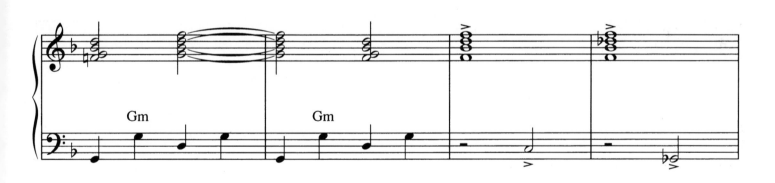

Consider Yourself
Words & Music by Lionel Bart

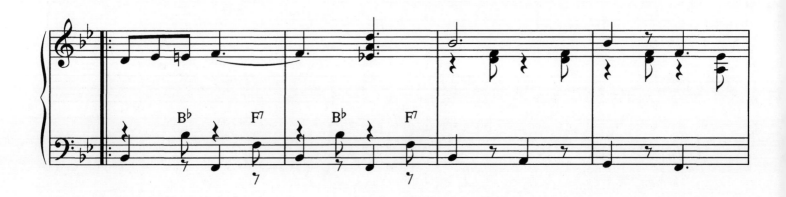

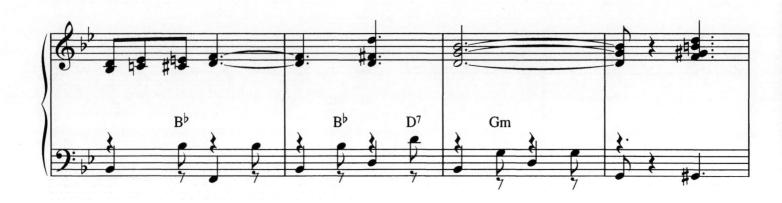

© Copyright 1959 by Lakeview Music Publishing Company Limited, Suite 2.07, Plaza 535 Kings Road, London SW10.
All Rights Reserved. International Copyright Secured.

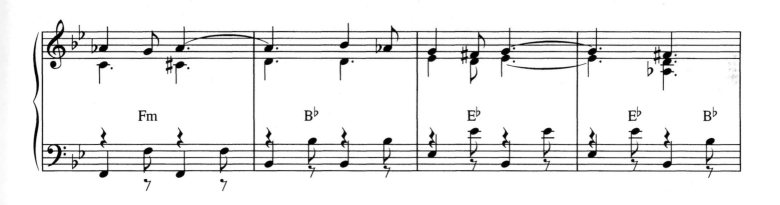
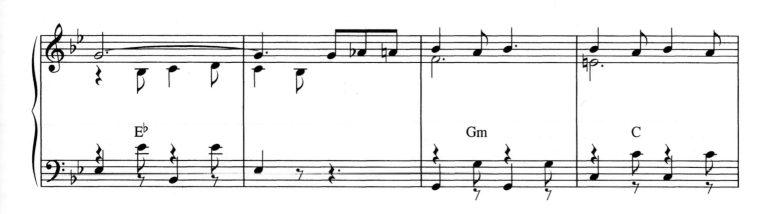

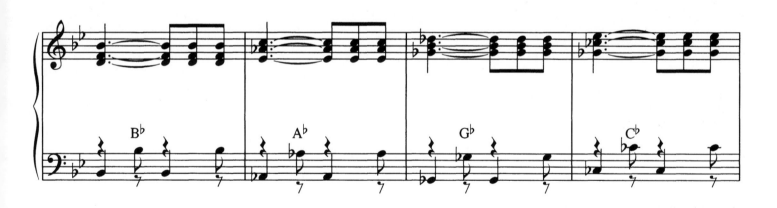
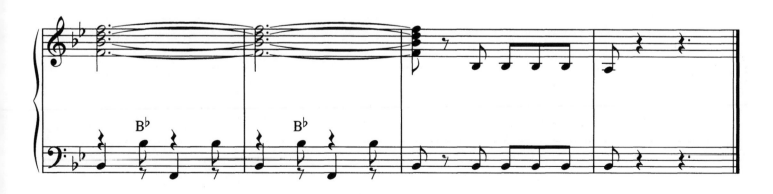

Can't Help Lovin' Dat Man
Music by Jerome Kern ◆ Words by Oscar Hammerstein II

© Copyright 1927 T. B. Harms & Company Incorporated, USA.
PolyGram Music Publishing Limited, 47 British Grove, London W4.
All Rights Reserved. International Copyright Secured.

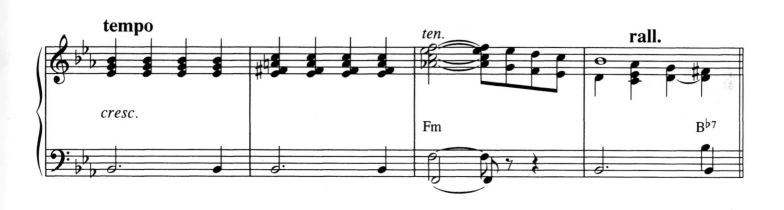

Climb Ev'ry Mountain
Words by Oscar Hammerstein II ◆ Music by Richard Rodgers

© Copyright 1959 and 1960 by Richard Rodgers and the Estate of Oscar Hammerstein II. Williamson Music Company, owner of publication and allied rights for all countries of the Western Hemisphere and Japan. Williamson Music Limited, for all countries of the Eastern Hemisphere (except Japan).
This arrangement © Copyright 1998 by Williamson Music Limited, used by Music Sales Limited with permission.
All Rights Reserved. International Copyright Secured.

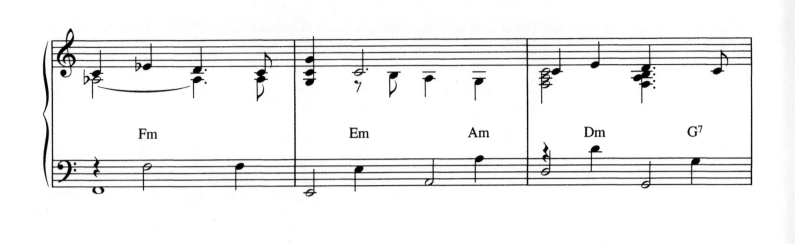

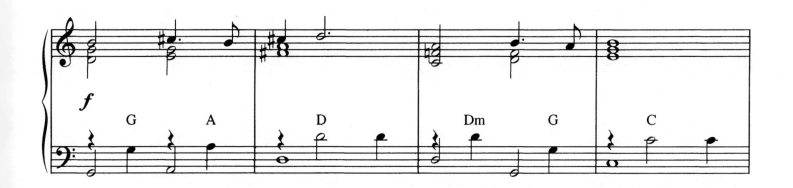
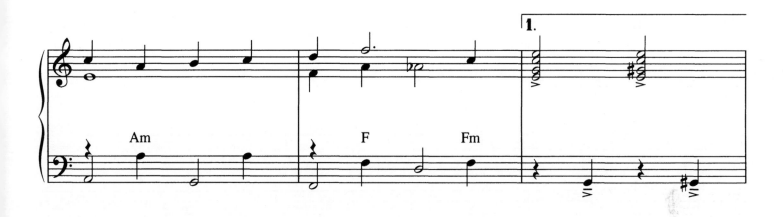
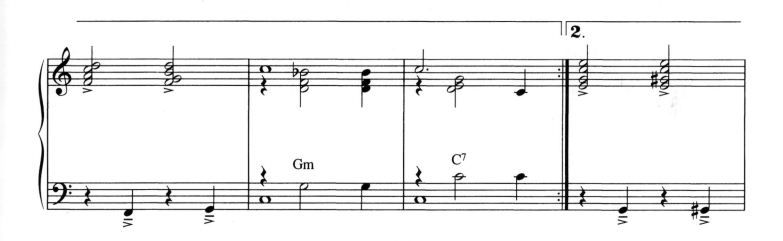
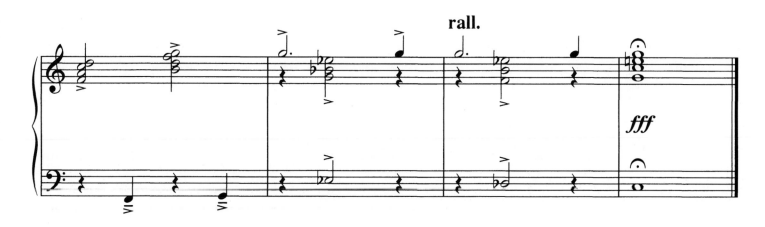

Ol' Man River
Music by Jerome Kern ◆ Words by Oscar Hammerstein II

© Copyright 1927 T. B. Harms & Company Incorporated, USA.
PolyGram Music Publishing Limited, 47 British Grove, London W4.
All Rights Reserved. International Copyright Secured.

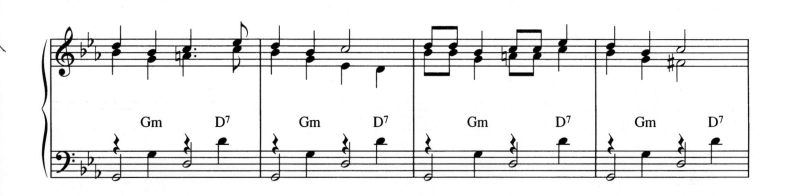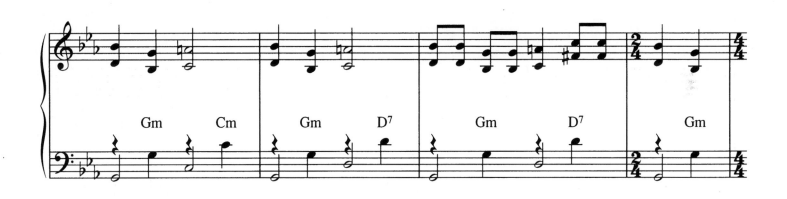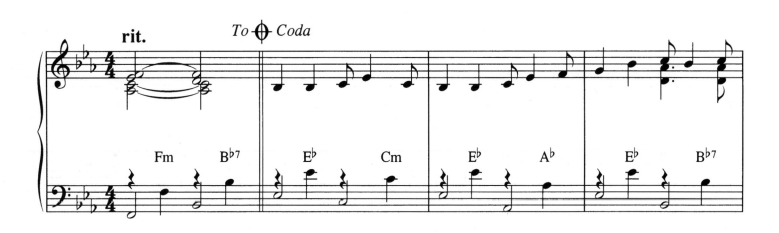

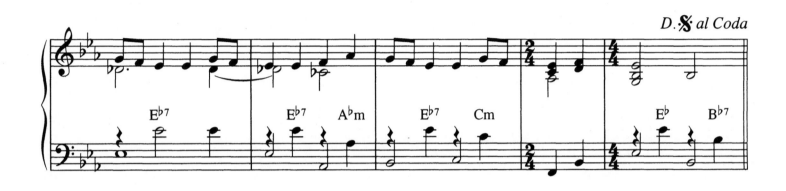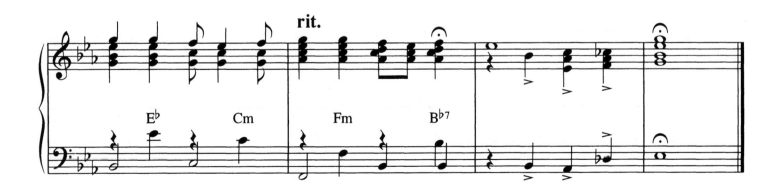

Seventy Six Trombones
Words & Music by Meredith Willson

© Copyright 1950, 1954 & 1957 Frank Music Corporation, USA.
© Renewed 1978, 1982 Frank Music Corporation & Meredith Willson Music.
Published & administered by MPL Communications Limited.
All Rights Reserved. International Copyright Secured.

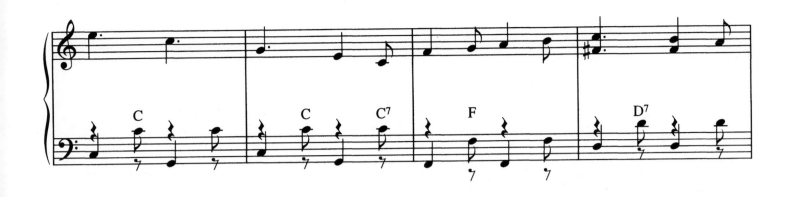

Hello, Young Lovers
Words by Oscar Hammerstein II ◆ Music by Richard Rodgers

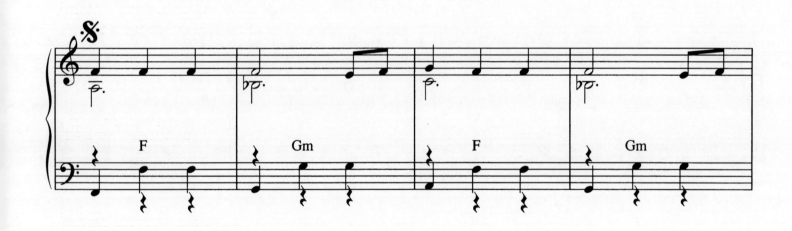

Till There Was You
Words & Music by Meredith Willson

© Copyright 1950, 1954 & 1957 Frank Music Corporation, USA.
© Renewed 1978, 1982 Frank Music Corporation & Meredith Willson Music.
Published & administered by MPL Communications Limited.
All Rights Reserved. International Copyright Secured.

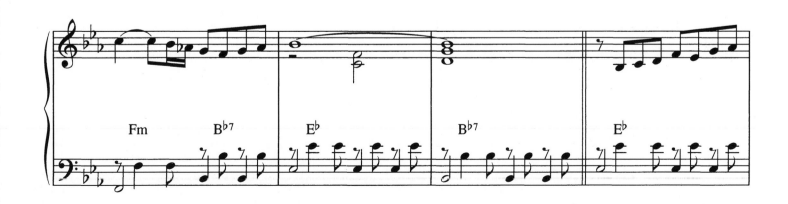

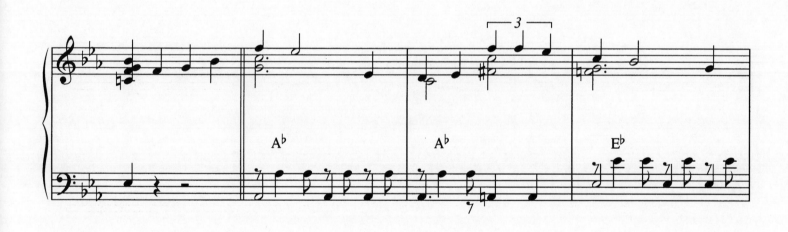

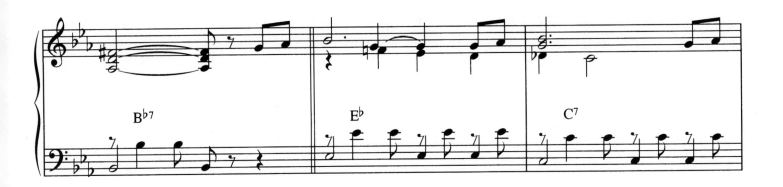

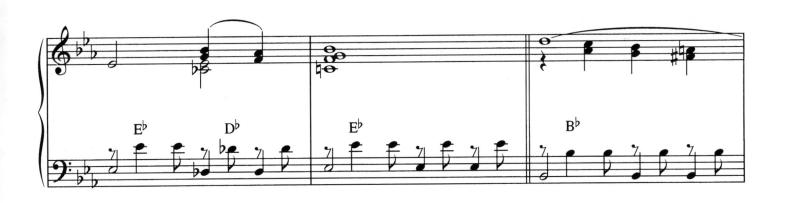

45

What I Did For Love
Words by Edward Kleban ◆ Music by Marvin Hamlisch

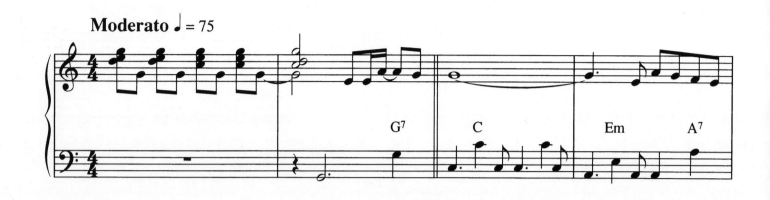

© Copyright 1975 Marvin Hamlisch and Edward Kleban.
All rights controlled by Wren Music Company Incorporated and American Compass Music Corporation.
Larry Shayne Enterprises Limited/Chappell Music Limited, London W6.
All Rights Reserved. International Copyright Secured.